A VEGETARIAN PREGNANCY COOKBOOK

NOURISHING YOUR JOURNEY

Veddet

For Cam to make sure
Sophie is nourished for
Little Miss Noble

love from nosey old Gran.
xxx

Copyright © [2023] by [Veddet]

All rights reserved. No part of this publication may be reproduced, distributed, or transmitted in any form or by any means, including photocopying, recording, or other electronic or mechanical methods, without the prior written permission of the publisher, except in the case of brief quotations embodied in critical reviews and certain other noncommercial uses permitted by copyright law.

This book is a work of non-fiction. Names, characters, places, and incidents either are products of the author's imagination or are used fictitiously. Any resemblance to actual persons, living or dead, events, or locales is entirely coincidental.

TABLE OF CONTENT

INTRODUCTION 5

CHAPTER 1 10

   THE VEGETARIAN PREGNANCY JOURNEY 10

      1.1 The Benefits of a Vegetarian Diet During Pregnancy 10

      1.2 Common Myths and Misconceptions 13

Chapter 2 16

   Building a Balanced Vegetarian Diet 16

      2.1 Essential Nutrients for Pregnancy 16

      2.2 Meal Planning and Portion Control 34

      2.3 Vegetarian Food Sources for Key Nutrients 37

Chapter 3 43

   Morning Sickness Solutions 43

      3-1 Coping with Nausea and Vomiting 43

      3.2 Nourishing Recipes for Queasy Days 47

Chapter 4 52

   Delicious and Nutrient-Packed Breakfasts 52

      4.1 Energizing Smoothies and Bowls 52

      4.2 Hearty Breakfast Tacos 58

      4.3 Baked Oatmeal Varieties 61

CHAPTER 5 66

   Wholesome Lunchtime Favorites 66

      5.1 Vibrant Salad Creations 66

      5.2 Satisfying Sandwiches and Wraps 72

      5.3 Hearty Soups and Stews 78

CHAPTER 6 83

Nutrient-Rich Dinners for Two 83

6.1 Flavorful Pasta Dishes 83

6.2 Protein-Packed Entrees 89

6.2 Protein-Packed Entrees 94

6.3 Veggie-Loaded Stir-Fries 99

CHAPTER 7 104

Snacks and Small Bites.. 104

7.1 Quick and Healthy Snack Ideas 104

7.2 Homemade Energy Bars and Bites 108

CHAPTER 8 113

Sweet Treats for Expecting Moms.. 113

8.1 Dessert Options without Guilt 113

8.2 Decadent Fruit-Based Sweets.. 117

CHAPTER 9 121

Staying Hydrated with Pregnancy-Friendly Drinks 121

9.1 Infused Water and Herbal Teas 121

9.2 Pregnancy Smoothies... 125

CHAPTER 11.. 130

Resources and Further Reading... 130

11.1 Recommended Cookbooks 130

11.2 Online Resources for Vegetarian Moms................................. 133

INTRODUCTION

Sarah had always been a dedicated vegetarian, choosing to nourish her body with the bountiful gifts of the earth. She believed in the power of plant-based foods not only to sustain her but also to provide the best possible foundation for her growing family.

Sarah's dream of becoming a mother had finally come true. She was expecting her first child, a tiny miracle that filled her heart with joy and anticipation.

But Sarah knew that this journey was about more than just her own health—it was about nurturing a new life, and she was determined to do it right.

Throughout her pregnancy, Sarah carefully crafted her vegetarian diet to ensure she received all the necessary nutrients.

She researched, consulted with nutritionists, and found creative ways to incorporate essential vitamins and minerals into her meals. Her mornings began with colorful smoothies packed with spinach, berries, and chia seeds. She enjoyed hearty salads filled with leafy greens, nuts, and a rainbow of vegetables for lunch. Dinners were a celebration of diverse cuisines, from Indian lentil dals to Mexican bean burritos, all bursting with flavor and nutrients.

Despite the occasional morning sickness, Sarah persisted. She understood that these challenges were a small price to pay for the health of her baby.

Her dedication to her vegetarian lifestyle and her baby's well-being fueled her determination.

As her due date approached, Sarah's doctor marveled at her vibrant health. Her energy levels were high, and her body showed no signs of nutrient deficiencies.

Sarah's commitment to her vegetarian diet had not only sustained her but had also given her baby the best possible start in life.

The day finally arrived when Sarah went into labor. She and her partner, Michael, rushed to the hospital, their hearts filled with excitement and a touch of nervousness. The labor was long and intense, but Sarah drew strength from the plant-based diet that had nourished her throughout her pregnancy.

She remembered the colorful meals, the nutrient-rich snacks, and the vibrant smoothies that had become a daily ritual.

After hours of hard work and determination, Sarah gave birth to a healthy baby girl.

The room filled with joy as the newborn took her first breath, and Sarah held her precious daughter in her arms, tears of happiness streaming down her face.

The little one was perfect, a testament to Sarah's unwavering dedication to her vegetarian lifestyle and her commitment to providing the best possible start in life.

As Sarah cradled her baby, she knew that her vegetarian journey had not only enriched her own life but had also paved the way for a healthy, vibrant future for her daughter. Together, they would continue to explore the world of plant-based cuisine, sharing the love of wholesome, nourishing food that had brought them to this beautiful moment

Bringing a new life into the world is a remarkable journey filled with anticipation, wonder, and joy.

Pregnancy is a time of transformation, not just for your body but also for your relationship with food. As you embark on this beautiful voyage, your dietary choices take on new significance, as they nourish not only you but also the precious life growing within you.

Welcome to "Nourishing Bites: A Vegetarian Pregnancy Cookbook.

" This book is a labor of love, designed to empower expecting mothers with the knowledge and culinary inspiration needed to maintain a balanced and nourishing vegetarian diet throughout pregnancy.

Whether you're a long-time vegetarian, a recent convert to a plant-based lifestyle, or simply someone looking to incorporate more meatless meals into your pregnancy journey, this cookbook is your trusted companion.

Throughout the book, you'll find an abundance of mouthwatering recipes, practical tips, and nutritional guidance to help you navigate the unique dietary challenges and opportunities of pregnancy while embracing the wonderful world of vegetarian cuisine.

As you turn the pages of "Nourishing Bites," my hope is that you'll not only discover new and exciting flavors but also deepen your connection with your body and the life growing within you.

Remember, this is a time to celebrate, savor, and nourish both your body and soul.

Let's embark on this journey together, one nourishing bite at a time.

With warmth and best wishes, [Veddet]

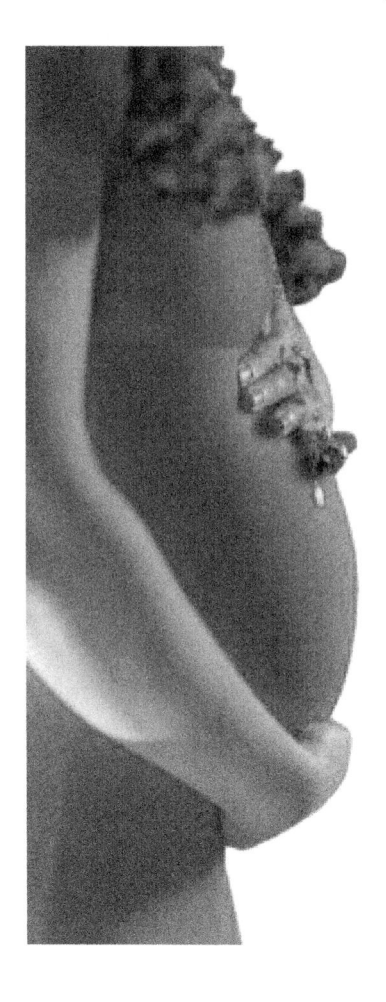

CHAPTER 1

THE VEGETARIAN PREGNANCY JOURNEY

1.1 The Benefits of a Vegetarian Diet During Pregnancy

A vegetarian diet during pregnancy can offer numerous benefits for both the expectant mother and her developing baby.

While it's essential to plan meals carefully to ensure proper nutrition, when done right, a vegetarian diet can provide a wide array of advantages:

Rich in Essential Nutrients: A well-balanced vegetarian diet is often rich in essential nutrients required during pregnancy. These include vitamins such as folate (critical for fetal development), vitamin C, vitamin A, and minerals like iron, calcium, and magnesium.

High in Fiber: Vegetarian diets typically include a significant amount of fiber from fruits, vegetables, whole grains, and legumes. This can help prevent constipation, a common discomfort during pregnancy.A vegetarian diet during pregnancy can offer numerous benefits for both the expectant mother and her developing baby.

While it's essential to plan meals carefully to ensure proper nutrition, when done right, a vegetarian diet can provide a wide array of advantages:

Rich in Essential Nutrients: A well-balanced vegetarian diet is often rich in essential nutrients required during pregnancy. These include vitamins such as folate (critical for fetal development), vitamin C, vitamin A, and minerals like iron, calcium, and magnesium.

High in Fiber: Vegetarian diets typically include a significant amount of fiber from fruits, vegetables, whole grains, and legumes. This can help prevent constipation, a common discomfort during pregnancy.

Low in Saturated Fat: Many vegetarian diets are naturally low in saturated fats, which can be beneficial for heart health during pregnancy. It can help maintain healthy cholesterol levels.

Reduced Risk of Gestational Diabetes: Some studies suggest that vegetarians may have a lower risk of developing gestational diabetes during pregnancy due to their typically lower intake of animal fats and higher intake of complex carbohydrates.

Healthy Weight Management: A vegetarian diet can support healthy weight management during pregnancy, helping to prevent excessive weight gain, which can reduce the risk of complications like gestational hypertension and pre-eclampsia.

Lower Risk of Preterm Birth: Some research indicates that vegetarian diets may be associated with a reduced risk of preterm birth, though more studies are needed to confirm this link.

Reduced Exposure to Environmental Toxins: Plant-based diets tend to have lower levels of environmental contaminants that can be found in animal products, such as mercury and PCBs.

Lower Cholesterol Levels: Vegetarian diets can help maintain or lower cholesterol levels, which is beneficial for heart health and can reduce the risk of cardiovascular complications during pregnancy.

Promotes a Variety of Foods: Vegetarian diets encourage a wide range of food choices, which can contribute to diverse nutrient intake and help ensure a broader spectrum of essential nutrients.

Ethical and Environmental Considerations: For many expectant mothers, choosing a vegetarian diet during pregnancy aligns with their ethical beliefs regarding animal welfare, and it can have a positive environmental impact by reducing the demand for meat production.

While there are many benefits to a vegetarian diet during pregnancy, it's crucial to emphasize proper planning and nutritional awareness. Pregnant vegetarians should ensure they are meeting their increased calorie and nutrient needs.

Consulting with a healthcare provider or a registered dietitian who specializes in prenatal nutrition is highly recommended to create a personalized meal plan that addresses specific dietary requirements during pregnancy, including adequate protein, iron, calcium, and omega-3 fatty acids.

This way, expectant mothers can enjoy the benefits of a vegetarian diet while providing optimal nourishment for themselves and their developing baby.

1.2 Common Myths and Misconceptions

When it comes to vegetarian diets during pregnancy, several common myths and misconceptions persist. It's important to dispel these myths to provide accurate information and support expectant mothers in making informed dietary choices. Here are some of the most prevalent myths and the truths that counter them:

Myth 1: Vegetarian Diets Lack Protein

Truth: Vegetarian diets can provide ample protein when well-planned. Plant-based protein sources like legumes, tofu, tempeh, quinoa, nuts, and seeds are rich in protein. Pregnant women can easily meet their protein needs with these foods.

Myth 2: Vegetarian Diets Don't Provide Enough Iron

Truth: Vegetarian diets can be a good source of iron. While plant-based iron (non-heme iron) is not as readily absorbed as heme iron from animal sources, consuming iron-rich foods with vitamin C-rich foods (like citrus fruits or bell peppers) can enhance iron absorption. Vegetarian sources of iron include beans, lentils, spinach, fortified cereals, and dried fruits.

Myth 3: Vegetarian Diets Are Deficient in Calcium

Truth: There are plenty of plant-based sources of calcium. Foods like fortified plant milk, tofu, leafy greens (such as kale and collard greens), almonds, and calcium-fortified foods are excellent options for maintaining healthy calcium levels during pregnancy.

Myth 4: Vegetarian Diets Are Low in Omega-3 Fatty Acids

Truth: While fish is a primary source of omega-3 fatty acids (particularly DHA and EPA), vegetarians can obtain these essential fats from plant-based sources like flaxseeds, chia seeds, hemp seeds, and walnuts. Some foods are also full with omega-3s.

Myth 5: Pregnant Vegetarians Lack Vitamin B12

Truth: Vitamin B12 is primarily found in animal products, so vegetarians should ensure they get enough from fortified foods (such as plant milk and breakfast cereals) or supplements. Vitamin B12 is essential for neurological development and preventing anemia.

Myth 6: Vegetarian Diets Are Inadequate for Fetal Development

Truth: A well-planned vegetarian diet can provide all the essential nutrients needed for fetal development. Pregnant vegetarians should focus on a diverse and balanced intake of foods, including a variety of fruits, vegetables, grains, legumes, and plant-based protein sources.

Myth 7: Vegetarian Diets Cause Birth Defects

Truth: There is no evidence to suggest that properly planned vegetarian diets cause birth defects. In fact, a balanced vegetarian diet can contribute to a healthy pregnancy and lower the risk of certain birth defects.

Myth 8: Vegetarian Diets Lead to Low Birth Weight Babies

Truth: When adequately nourished, pregnant vegetarians can give birth to healthy babies with normal birth weights. A well-balanced vegetarian diet that meets calorie and nutrient needs can support healthy fetal growth.

It's important for pregnant vegetarians to consult with a healthcare provider or registered dietitian who specializes in prenatal nutrition to ensure they are meeting their specific dietary requirements. Proper planning and nutritional awareness can help expectant mothers enjoy the benefits of a vegetarian diet while providing optimal nourishment for themselves and their developing baby, dispelling these common myths and misconceptions along the way.

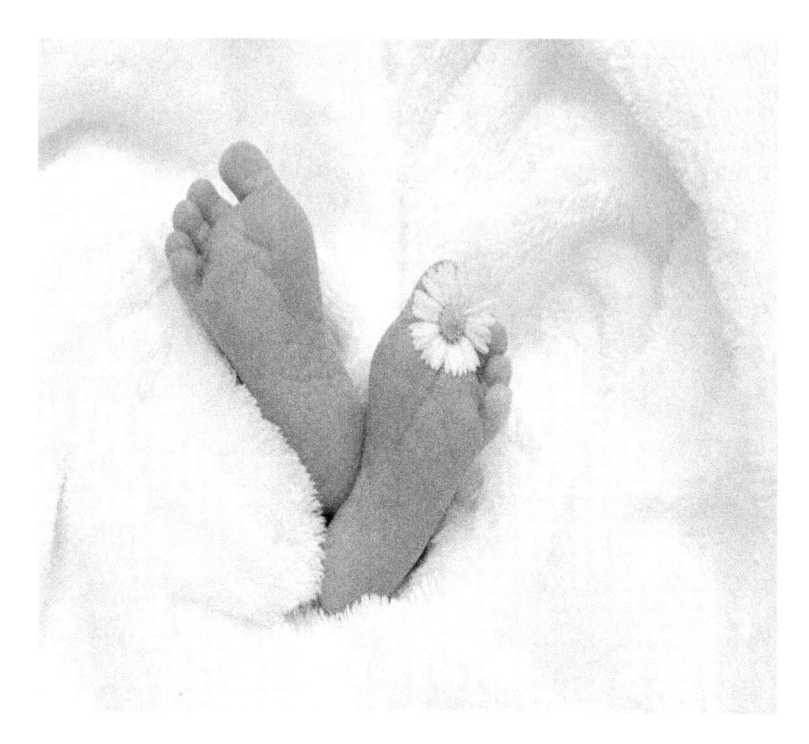

Chapter 2

Building a Balanced Vegetarian Diet

2.1 Essential Nutrients for Pregnancy

During pregnancy, ensuring you receive essential nutrients is crucial for your health and the healthy development of your baby. A well-balanced diet that provides these essential nutrients is essential. Here are some of the most important nutrients during pregnancy:

Folate (Folic Acid): Folate is vital for preventing neural tube defects in the developing fetus. It is found in foods like leafy greens, fortified cereals, beans, and lentils. Most prenatal vitamins also contain folic acid.

Iron: Iron is needed for the production of red blood cells to transport oxygen to your baby.

Good sources of iron include lean meats, poultry, fish, fortified cereals, beans, and spinach. Vitamin C-rich foods can enhance iron absorption.

Calcium: Calcium is essential for the development of your baby's bones and teeth, as well as for maintaining your own bone health. Dairy products (if you're not vegan), calcium-fortified plant-based milk, tofu, and leafy greens are good sources.

Protein: Protein is essential for the growth of the baby's cells and tissues. Incorporate sources like beans, lentils, tofu, nuts, seeds, and lean meats or plant-based protein alternatives into your diet.

Omega-3 Fatty Acids: Omega-3s, particularly DHA, are crucial for the development of your baby's brain and eyes. Sources include fatty fish (like salmon), flaxseeds, chia seeds, walnuts, and algae-based supplements.

Vitamin D: Vitamin D helps your body absorb calcium and supports the baby's bone development.

It can be obtained from sun exposure, fortified foods (like fortified cereals and plant-based milk), and supplements as recommended by your healthcare provider.

Vitamin A: Vitamin A is necessary for the baby's vision, skin, and tissue development. It can be found in foods like sweet potatoes, carrots, dark leafy greens, and apricots.

Vitamin C: Vitamin C helps your body absorb iron and aids in tissue repair. Citrus fruits, strawberries, bell peppers, and broccoli are excellent sources.

Vitamin B12: Vitamin B12 is essential for neurological development and preventing anemia. It is primarily found in animal products, so vegetarians should ensure they get enough from fortified foods or supplements.

Zinc: Zinc supports the baby's growth and the immune system. Good sources include beans, nuts, whole grains, and dairy products (if you're not vegan).

Iodine: Iodine is vital for the baby's brain development and thyroid function. It can be found in iodized salt, seafood, and dairy products (if you're not vegan).

Choline: Choline supports brain development and helps prevent certain birth defects. Eggs, soybeans, and broccoli are sources of choline.

Fiber: Adequate fiber intake can help prevent constipation, a common discomfort during pregnancy. Fiber-rich foods include fruits, vegetables, whole grains, and legumes.

Remember, every pregnancy is unique, and individual nutrient needs may vary. It's essential to consult with your healthcare provider or a registered dietitian who specializes in prenatal nutrition to create a personalized meal plan that addresses your specific dietary requirements during pregnancy. They can help you make sure you're getting all the essential nutrients necessary for a healthy pregnancy

Protein

Protein is one of the essential macronutrients required for the proper functioning of the human body. It plays a crucial role during pregnancy, supporting both the mother's health and the growth and development of the fetus. Here's why protein is important during pregnancy:

Fatal Growth and Development: Protein is a building block for cells and tissues, and it is especially critical for the development of the baby's organs, muscles, and tissues. Adequate protein intake supports healthy fatal growth.

Placenta and Amniotic Fluid: The placenta and amniotic fluid, which surround and nourish the fetus, also require protein for their formation and function. Protein helps ensure a healthy environment for the baby.

Blood Volume Expansion: During pregnancy, a woman's blood volume increases to supply oxygen and nutrients to the developing fetus. Protein plays a role in maintaining and expanding blood volume.

Maternal Tissue Growth and Repair: Protein is essential for the growth and repair of the mother's tissues, including her uterus and breasts. It helps prepare the body for childbirth and breastfeeding.

Immune System Support: Protein is a key component of the immune system. During pregnancy, when the immune system is naturally suppressed to protect the fetus, maintaining adequate protein intake can help support immune function.

Preventing Edema: Edema, or swelling, is common during pregnancy due to increased fluid retention. Adequate protein intake can help regulate fluid balance and reduce the severity of edema.

Muscle Maintenance: Protein helps maintain muscle mass, which is important for overall strength and mobility during pregnancy. It also supports the muscles used during labor and delivery.

To ensure you get enough protein during pregnancy, consider including a variety of protein-rich foods in your diet, such as:

Legumes: Beans, lentils, and chickpeas are excellent sources of plant-based protein.

Tofu and Tempeh: These soy-based products are versatile protein sources.

Nuts and Seeds: Almonds, peanuts, chia seeds, and hemp seeds are protein-rich options.

Dairy or Dairy Alternatives: Milk, yogurt, and cheese (if you're not vegan) provide protein and calcium.

Eggs: Eggs are a complete protein source and contain essential nutrients.

Lean Meats and Poultry: If you're not vegetarian, lean meats and poultry are rich in protein.

Fish: Fatty fish like salmon also provide protein and omega-3 fatty acids.

Whole Grains: While not as protein-dense as other sources, whole grains like quinoa and whole wheat pasta contribute to overall protein intake.

It's important to consult with your healthcare provider or a registered dietitian during pregnancy to determine your specific protein needs, as they may vary based on your individual circumstances. They can help you create a balanced meal plan that ensures you receive adequate protein to support both your health and the growth and development of your baby.

Folate

Folate, also known as vitamin B9, is a crucial nutrient, especially during pregnancy. It plays a vital role in the development of the baby's neural tube, which eventually forms the brain and spinal cord. Here's why folate is important during pregnancy:

Neural Tube Development: Folate is essential for the formation and closure of the neural tube, which occurs in the early weeks of pregnancy. A deficiency in folate during this critical period can lead to neural tube defects, such as spina bifida and anencephaly, which can cause severe lifelong disabilities or even be fatal.

Cell Division and DNA Synthesis: Folate is involved in DNA synthesis and cell division, making it important for the growth and development of all cells, including those of the developing fetus.

Red Blood Cell Formation: Folate is necessary for the production of red blood cells. During pregnancy, a woman's blood volume increases to support the growing fetus, so an adequate supply of folate is essential to prevent anemia.

Prevention of Other Birth Defects: In addition to neural tube defects, folate may also help prevent other birth defects, including heart defects, cleft palate, and certain congenital heart diseases.

To ensure you get enough folate during pregnancy, consider the following sources:

Folate-Rich Foods: Leafy greens (such as spinach and kale), broccoli, asparagus, and Brussels sprouts are excellent sources of folate.

Legumes: Beans (like lentils and black beans) and peas are high in folate.

Citrus Fruits: Oranges and orange juice, as well as other citrus fruits, are good sources of folate.

Fortified Foods: Many breakfast cereals and grain products (like bread and pasta) are fortified with folic acid, a synthetic form of folate.

Supplements: Prenatal vitamins typically contain the recommended amount of folate. Your healthcare provider may also recommend a folic acid supplement, especially if you have a higher risk of deficiency.

During pregnancy, the recommended daily intake of folate is 600-800 micrograms (mcg) of dietary folate equivalents (DFE).

It's essential to begin getting enough folate even before conception since the neural tube forms in the early weeks of pregnancy, often before a woman knows she's pregnant.

It's recommended that pregnant women consult with their healthcare provider to ensure they are meeting their specific folate needs. Some women may require higher doses of folate if they have certain risk factors or medical conditions. Adequate folate intake is a simple yet crucial step to help ensure a healthy pregnancy and a healthy baby

Iron

Iron is an essential mineral that plays a vital role during pregnancy. It's responsible for carrying oxygen in the blood, and its importance becomes even more pronounced when you're expecting. Here's why iron is crucial during pregnancy:

Preventing Anemia: Iron deficiency anemia is a common concern during pregnancy. As your blood volume increases to support the growing fetus, your body needs more iron to produce the necessary red blood cells.

Anemia can lead to fatigue, weakness, and other health complications, which can be harmful during pregnancy.

Fetal Growth and Development: Iron is essential for the development of the baby's organs and tissues. Adequate iron intake helps ensure that the fetus receives enough oxygen and nutrients for healthy growth.

Placental and Uterine Development: Iron supports the development of the placenta and uterus, critical for a healthy pregnancy.

Immune Function: Iron is necessary for a well-functioning immune system, which helps protect both the mother and the developing fetus from infections and illnesses.

Preventing Preterm Birth and Low Birth Weight: Iron deficiency during pregnancy has been associated with an increased risk of preterm birth and low birth weight, which can have long-term health consequences for the baby.

To ensure you get enough iron during pregnancy, consider the following sources:

Lean Meats: Red meat, poultry, and fish are excellent sources of heme iron, which is more easily absorbed by the body.

Plant-Based Sources: Legumes (such as lentils and chickpeas), tofu, tempeh, fortified cereals, and beans are rich in non-heme iron, which is less readily absorbed but can be improved with vitamin C-rich foods.

Leafy Greens: Spinach, kale, and collard greens contain non-heme iron.

Dried Fruits: Prunes, apricots, and raisins are good sources of iron.

Nuts and Seeds: Almonds, pumpkin seeds, and sunflower seeds provide iron.

Iron Supplements: Prenatal vitamins often include iron. If your healthcare provider determines you need additional supplementation, they may prescribe an iron supplement.

It's crucial to consult with your healthcare provider to determine your specific iron needs during pregnancy. They may recommend iron supplements if you are at risk of deficiency or if your blood tests show low iron levels.

To enhance iron absorption, pair iron-rich foods with vitamin C-rich foods like citrus fruits, strawberries, or bell peppers. However, avoid consuming calcium-rich foods or supplements at the same time as iron-rich foods, as calcium can interfere with iron absorption.

Ensuring you receive sufficient iron during pregnancy is essential for your health and the well-being of your baby, helping to prevent anemia and supporting healthy fetal development.

Calcium

Calcium is an essential mineral that plays a crucial role during pregnancy, contributing to the overall health of both the mother and the developing baby. Here's why calcium is important during pregnancy:

Bone and Teeth Formation: Calcium is a primary building block for bones and teeth. During pregnancy, the baby's bones and teeth are developing rapidly, and calcium intake is vital to support this process.

Muscle Function: Calcium is necessary for proper muscle function, including the contractions of the heart and the muscles used during labor and delivery.

Blood Clotting: Calcium is involved in blood clotting, which is essential to prevent excessive bleeding during childbirth.

Nerve Transmission: Calcium plays a role in transmitting nerve signals, contributing to overall nerve function.

Maintenance of Maternal Bone Health: Pregnancy can increase the risk of maternal bone loss, as the developing baby draws calcium from the mother's bones. Adequate calcium intake can help prevent bone density loss during this time.

To ensure you get enough calcium during pregnancy, consider the following sources:

Dairy Products: Milk, yogurt, and cheese are rich sources of calcium. Opt for low-fat or fat-free varieties if you're concerned about excessive saturated fat intake.

Calcium-Fortified Foods: Many plant-based milk alternatives (such as almond milk, soy milk, and rice milk) and orange juice are fortified with calcium.

Be sure to choose fortified versions labeled as containing calcium.

Leafy Greens: Dark, leafy greens like collard greens, kale, and broccoli contain calcium, although the calcium absorption from these sources is lower compared to dairy products.

Tofu: Calcium-set tofu (calcium sulfate or calcium chloride) is a good source of calcium. Be sure to check the label for the calcium content.

Canned Fish: Fish with edible bones, such as canned salmon and sardines, provide a calcium boost.

Supplements: Prenatal vitamins often include calcium. If you're concerned about meeting your calcium needs through diet alone, your healthcare provider may recommend a calcium supplement.

During pregnancy, the recommended daily intake of calcium for most pregnant women is around 1,000-1,300 milligrams (mg), depending on age and other factors.

It's important to consult with your healthcare provider to determine your specific calcium needs and to ensure you are getting an appropriate amount.

Remember that calcium absorption can be influenced by other dietary factors. For example, calcium absorption is enhanced by vitamin D, so ensure you are also meeting your vitamin D needs, either through diet, sunlight exposure, or supplements as recommended by your healthcare provider.

Adequate calcium intake during pregnancy supports both the mother's health and the healthy development of the baby's bones and teeth, making it a vital nutrient to prioritize during this time.

Omega-3 fatty acids

Omega-3 fatty acids are essential polyunsaturated fats that offer numerous health benefits during pregnancy, playing a critical role in the development of both the mother and the baby. Here's why omega-3 fatty acids are important during pregnancy:

Fetal Brain Development: Omega-3 fatty acids, particularly docosahexaenoic acid (DHA), are essential for the development of the baby's brain and nervous system. These fats help build the brain's structure and function, supporting cognitive and visual development.

Eye Development: DHA also contributes to the development of the baby's eyes, particularly the retina. It plays a role in visual acuity and may help prevent vision problems.

Anti-Inflammatory Properties: Omega-3 fatty acids have anti-inflammatory properties, which can help reduce inflammation in the mother's body, supporting overall health and potentially reducing the risk of pregnancy complications related to inflammation.

Heart Health: Omega-3s have been associated with a reduced risk of heart disease and may help maintain cardiovascular health during pregnancy, particularly in women with certain risk factors.

Preventing Preterm Birth: Some studies suggest that omega-3 supplementation during pregnancy may reduce the risk of preterm birth and low birth weight, although more research is needed in this area.

To ensure you get enough omega-3 fatty acids during pregnancy, consider the following sources:

Fatty Fish: Fatty fish like salmon, mackerel, sardines, and trout are among the best sources of omega-3s, particularly DHA and EPA (eicosapentaenoic acid).

Algae-Based Supplements: If you're vegetarian or vegan, you can obtain DHA from algae-based supplements, as fish obtain their omega-3s from algae.

Flaxseeds: Ground flaxseeds are a good plant-based source of omega-3s, specifically alpha-linolenic acid (ALA). However, ALA is not as potent as DHA and EPA.

Chia Seeds: Chia seeds also provide ALA, making them a nutritious addition to your diet.

Walnuts: Walnuts contain ALA and can be included in salads, oatmeal, or as a snack.

During pregnancy, it's important to consume a balanced and varied diet that includes omega-3-rich foods.

However, because the body's ability to convert ALA (from plant sources) into DHA and EPA is limited, pregnant women should aim to include fatty fish in their diet or consider an algae-based DHA supplement if they don't consume fish. Discussing your omega-3 intake with your healthcare provider is a good idea, as they can provide personalized recommendations based on your dietary preferences and specific needs.

2.2 Meal Planning and Portion Control

Meal planning and portion control are essential components of maintaining a healthy and balanced diet during pregnancy.

Proper planning ensures that you receive the necessary nutrients to support your health and the growth of your baby while preventing excessive weight gain. Here are some tips on meal planning and portion control during pregnancy:

1. Create a Balanced Meal Plan:

Consult with a healthcare provider or registered dietitian to determine your specific dietary needs during pregnancy. Factors like your age, weight, activity level, and any medical conditions will influence your nutritional requirements.

Develop a meal plan that includes a variety of foods from all food groups. This should encompass fruits, vegetables, whole grains, lean proteins, and dairy or dairy alternatives (if you're not vegan).

Aim for three balanced meals and two to three snacks each day to maintain stable energy levels and help prevent overeating.

2. Focus on Nutrient-Rich Foods:

Prioritize nutrient-dense foods that provide essential vitamins and minerals, such as folate, iron, calcium, and omega-3 fatty acids.

Include lean sources of protein like poultry, fish, tofu, legumes, and beans in your meals.

Choose whole grains like brown rice, quinoa, and whole wheat bread to increase fiber intake and provide sustained energy.

3. Watch Portion Sizes:

Pay attention to portion sizes to prevent excessive calorie intake and weight gain. Use measuring cups, a food scale, or visual cues to estimate appropriate portions.

Aim to fill half your plate with vegetables, one-quarter with lean protein, and one-quarter with whole grains.

Be mindful of high-calorie condiments and dressings, and use them sparingly.

4. Snack Wisely:

Opt for healthy, nutrient-rich snacks, such as yogurt with berries, a handful of nuts, or a piece of fruit with nut butter.

Avoid empty-calorie snacks like sugary drinks, chips, and candy.

5. Stay Hydrated:

Drink plenty of water throughout the day to stay hydrated. Dehydration can lead to overeating or cravings.

Limit caffeine intake, as excessive caffeine consumption may have adverse effects during pregnancy.

6. Listen to Your Body:

Pay attention to hunger and fullness cues. Eat when you're hungry and stop when you're satisfied.

Avoid skipping meals, as this can lead to overeating later in the day.

7. Avoid Emotional Eating:

Be mindful of emotional eating. Find non-food-related ways to cope with stress, anxiety, or other emotional triggers.

8. Consult a Professional:

If you have specific dietary concerns, consult a registered dietitian who specializes in prenatal nutrition.

They can help you create a personalized meal plan and provide guidance on portion control.

Remember that pregnancy is a unique journey, and your nutritional needs may vary. Regular communication with your healthcare provider and a balanced, portion-controlled meal plan can help ensure a healthy and comfortable pregnancy while providing the best possible nourishment for you and your baby.

2.3 Vegetarian Food Sources for Key Nutrients

Maintaining a balanced vegetarian diet during pregnancy requires careful consideration of key nutrients. Here are vegetarian food sources for essential nutrients important during pregnancy:

1. Protein:

Legumes (beans, lentils, chickpeas)

Tofu and tempeh

Quinoa

Nuts and seeds (almonds, peanuts, chia seeds, hemp seeds)

Eggs (if you're not vegan)

2. Folate (Folic Acid):

Leafy greens (spinach, kale, collard greens)

Fortified cereals and grains (look for products with added folic acid)

Legumes (lentils, chickpeas)

Avocado

Citrus fruits (oranges, grapefruits)

3. Iron:

Fortified cereals and grains

Legumes (lentils, chickpeas, black beans)

Dark leafy greens (spinach, kale)

Dried fruits (raisins, apricots)

Seeds (pumpkin seeds, sunflower seeds)

Tofu

Whole grains (quinoa, brown rice)

4. Calcium:

Dairy or dairy alternatives (calcium-fortified plant-based milk)

Leafy greens (collard greens, bok choy)

Tofu (if prepared with calcium sulfate or calcium chloride)

Almonds

Chia seeds

Fortified orange juice

5. Omega-3 Fatty Acids (DHA and EPA):

Algae-based supplements (if you're not consuming fatty fish)

Flaxseeds and flaxseed oil

Chia seeds

Walnuts

6. Vitamin D:

Sunlight exposure (limited)

Fortified foods (calcium-fortified plant-based milk, cereals)

Supplements (consult your healthcare provider for appropriate dosage)

7. Vitamin B12:

Fortified foods (breakfast cereals, plant-based milk, nutritional yeast)

Eggs (if you're not vegan)

Vitamin B12 supplements (particularly important for vegans)

8. Zinc:

Legumes (beans, lentils, chickpeas)

Nuts (cashews, almonds, peanuts)

Whole grains (oats, brown rice)

Dairy or dairy alternatives (if not vegan)

9. Vitamin A:

Sweet potatoes

Carrots

Dark leafy greens (spinach, kale)

Apricots

Mangoes

10. Vitamin C:

Citrus fruits (oranges, grapefruits)

Strawberries

Kiwi

Bell peppers

Broccoli

11. Fiber:

Whole grains (quinoa, whole wheat pasta)

Legumes (beans, lentils)

Fruits (apples, pears, berries)

Vegetables (carrots, broccoli, cauliflower)

Nuts and seeds

12. Choline:

Eggs (if you're not vegan)

Soy products (tofu, tempeh)

Legumes (chickpeas, lentils)

Whole grains (quinoa, brown rice)

Ensure that your vegetarian diet includes a variety of these nutrient-rich foods to meet your specific dietary requirements during pregnancy. If you have concerns about nutrient intake or have dietary restrictions, consult a healthcare provider or a registered dietitian who specializes in prenatal nutrition for personalized guidance and recommendations.

Chapter 3

Morning Sickness Solutions

3-1 Coping with Nausea and Vomiting

Nausea and vomiting, commonly referred to as morning sickness, can be a challenging symptom of pregnancy. While it's most common during the first trimester, some women may experience it throughout their pregnancy. Here are some strategies to cope with nausea and vomiting during pregnancy:

1. Eat Small, Frequent Meals:

Rather than three large meals, try eating five or six smaller meals throughout the day. An empty stomach can trigger nausea.

2. Choose Bland, Easily Digestible Foods:

Opt for plain foods like crackers, rice, plain toast, and applesauce. These can be easier on your stomach.

3. Ginger:

Ginger has natural anti-nausea properties. Consider ginger tea, ginger candies, or ginger ale (with real ginger). You can also try ginger supplements after consulting with your healthcare provider.

4. Stay Hydrated:

Sip fluids throughout the day to prevent dehydration. Clear fluids like water, herbal tea, and diluted fruit juices are good options.

5. Avoid Trigger Foods:

Identify foods or smells that trigger your nausea and try to avoid them.

6. Acupressure Wristbands:

Some women find relief from nausea by wearing acupressure wristbands.

7. Rest:

Fatigue can exacerbate nausea. Get plenty of rest and take naps as needed.

8. Fresh Air:

Take short walks or get fresh air to help alleviate nausea.

9. Prenatal Vitamins:

Sometimes prenatal vitamins can trigger nausea. Try taking them with food or before bed.

10. Aromatherapy:

Some scents, like lemon or peppermint, may help alleviate nausea. You can try inhaling them or using essential oils (ensure they're safe for pregnancy).

11. Medications:

If your nausea and vomiting are severe and impacting your ability to eat or stay hydrated, talk to your healthcare provider about medications that are safe during pregnancy.

12. Mindfulness and Relaxation Techniques:

Stress and anxiety can worsen nausea. Practicing relaxation techniques, such as deep breathing or prenatal yoga, may help.

13. Peppermint or Spearmint:

Peppermint or spearmint tea may help soothe nausea.

14. Ice Chips:

Sucking on ice chips or ice pops can help keep you hydrated.

Remember that every pregnancy is unique, and what works for one person may not work for another. It's essential to consult with your healthcare provider if you're experiencing severe or persistent nausea and vomiting, as they can provide personalized advice and treatment options. In some cases, severe morning sickness may require medical intervention to prevent dehydration and malnutrition.

3.2 Nourishing Recipes for Queasy Days

When you're experiencing nausea during pregnancy, finding nourishing and comforting recipes can be a real relief. Here are some gentle and nourishing recipe ideas for queasy days:

1. Ginger and Honey Tea:

Ingredients:

Fresh ginger slices

Honey

Hot water

Instructions:

Steep fresh ginger slices in hot water for a few minutes.

Sweeten with honey if desired.

Sip this soothing tea throughout the day to ease nausea.

2. Toasted Rice Soup:

Ingredients:

1/2 cup white rice

6 cups vegetable or chicken broth

Salt and pepper to taste

Instructions:

Rinse the rice under cold water until the water runs clear.

Toast the rice in a dry pot over medium heat until it turns slightly golden.

Add the broth, bring to a boil, then reduce heat and simmer until the rice is cooked.

Season with salt and pepper.

3. Mashed Potatoes with Avocado:

Ingredients:

2 large potatoes, peeled and diced

1 ripe avocado

Salt and pepper to taste

Instructions:

Boil the potatoes until tender, then drain.

Mash the potatoes and mix in the ripe avocado.

Season with salt and pepper.

Avocado adds creaminess and healthy fats.

4. Banana Oatmeal Smoothie:

Ingredients:

1 ripe banana

1/2 cup oats

1 cup almond milk or yogurt

1 tablespoon honey (optional)

Instructions:

Blend all ingredients until smooth.

Oats provide fiber, and banana offers potassium.

5. Baked Apples with Cinnamon:

Ingredients:

2 apples, cored and sliced

1 teaspoon cinnamon

1 tablespoon honey (optional)

Instructions:

Toss the apple slices with cinnamon.

Place in a baking dish and drizzle with honey.

Bake at 350°F (175°C) for about 20 minutes or until tender.

Cinnamon may help alleviate nausea.

6. Vegetable Broth with Rice:

Ingredients:

6 cups vegetable broth

1/2 cup cooked rice

Chopped carrots and zucchini

Salt and pepper to taste

Instructions:

Simmer the vegetable broth with chopped vegetables until tender.

Add cooked rice and season with salt and pepper.

Vegetable broth provides hydration and nutrients.

7. Popsicles:

Ingredients:

Fruit juice (e.g., apple, orange, or ginger ale)

Instructions:

Pour fruit juice into popsicle molds or ice cube trays.

Freeze for a refreshing treat.

These recipes are gentle on the stomach and can provide nourishment when you're feeling queasy. Remember to listen to your body and choose foods that you can tolerate best during episodes of nausea. If nausea persists or becomes severe, consult your healthcare provider for further guidance.

Chapter 4

Delicious and Nutrient-Packed Breakfasts

4.1 Energizing Smoothies and Bowls

Energizing smoothies and bowls can be a great way to boost your energy and stay nourished during pregnancy. Here are some delicious and nutritious recipes:

1. Berry Blast Smoothie:

Ingredients:

1 cup mixed berries (strawberries, blueberries, raspberries)

1 banana

1/2 cup Greek yogurt

1 tablespoon honey (optional)

1/2 cup almond milk or orange juice

Ice cubes

Instructions:

Blend all ingredients until smooth.

Berries provide antioxidants, while Greek yogurt adds protein.

2. Green Power Smoothie:

Ingredients:

1 cup spinach or kale

1/2 banana

1/2 cup Greek yogurt

1 tablespoon almond butter

1/2 cup almond milk

1 tablespoon honey (optional)

Ice cubes

Instructions:

Blend all ingredients until smooth.

Leafy greens offer essential nutrients, and almond butter adds healthy fats.

3. Tropical Energy Bowl:

Ingredients:

1/2 cup mango chunks

1/2 cup pineapple chunks

1/2 banana

1/4 cup coconut milk

Toppings: sliced banana, shredded coconut, granola, and chia seeds

Instructions:

Blend mango, pineapple, banana, and coconut milk until smooth.

Pour into a bowl and add toppings for added texture and nutrients.

4. Peanut Butter Banana Bowl:

Ingredients:

1 banana

2 tablespoons peanut butter

1/2 cup Greek yogurt

1 tablespoon honey (optional)

Toppings: sliced banana, chopped nuts, and a drizzle of honey

Instructions:

Blend banana, peanut butter, Greek yogurt, and honey until smooth.

Top with banana slices, chopped nuts, and a drizzle of honey for extra energy.

5. Chia Pudding Bowl:

Ingredients:

1/4 cup chia seeds

1 cup almond milk

1/2 teaspoon vanilla extract

Fresh berries and sliced almonds for toppings

Instructions:

Mix chia seeds, almond milk, and vanilla extract in a bowl.

Let it sit in the refrigerator for a few hours or overnight until it thickens.

Top with fresh berries and sliced almonds for a nutritious and energy-packed bowl.

6. Banana Date Smoothie:

Ingredients:

2 ripe bananas

4-5 pitted dates

1/2 cup Greek yogurt

1/2 cup almond milk

1/2 teaspoon cinnamon

Ice cubes

Instructions:

Blend all ingredients until smooth.

Dates provide natural sweetness and energy.

These energizing smoothies and bowls are packed with essential nutrients, including vitamins, minerals, protein, and healthy fats, to help keep you energized and nourished during pregnancy. Feel free to customize them to your taste and dietary preferences.

4.2 Hearty Breakfast Tacos

Hearty breakfast tacos are a delicious and satisfying way to start your day during pregnancy. Here's a recipe for hearty breakfast tacos that are packed with protein and flavor:

Ingredients:

For the Filling:

4 large eggs

1/2 cup black beans, drained and rinsed

1/2 cup diced bell peppers (use a mix of colors for added vibrancy)

1/4 cup diced onions

1/2 cup diced tomatoes

1/2 cup grated cheddar cheese

1 tablespoon olive oil

Salt and pepper to taste

For the Tacos:

4 small whole-grain or corn tortillas

1/4 cup salsa (choose your preferred level of spiciness)

Fresh cilantro leaves for garnish (optional)

Avocado slices for garnish (optional)

Instructions:

Heat the olive oil in a skillet over medium heat.

Add the diced onions and bell peppers to the skillet. Sauté for about 2-3 minutes, or until they start to soften.

Stir in the black beans and diced tomatoes. Cook for an additional 2-3 minutes, allowing the flavors to meld. Season with a pinch of salt and pepper.

In a separate bowl, beat the eggs. Pour them into the skillet with the vegetable mixture.

Scramble the eggs with the vegetables until they are fully cooked and no longer runny.

Warm the tortillas in the microwave or in a dry skillet for about 10-15 seconds on each side.

To assemble the tacos, spoon the egg and vegetable mixture onto each tortilla.

Sprinkle grated cheddar cheese on top of the filling.

Add a dollop of salsa to each taco.

Garnish with fresh cilantro leaves and avocado slices if desired.

Fold the tortillas over the filling to create tacos.

These hearty breakfast tacos are not only packed with protein but also contain essential nutrients from the vegetables and whole-grain tortillas. They are a satisfying and delicious way to fuel your morning and keep your energy levels up during pregnancy. Enjoy!

4.3 Baked Oatmeal Varieties

Baked oatmeal is a versatile and comforting breakfast dish that can be customized to suit your taste preferences and dietary needs during pregnancy. Here are several delicious varieties of baked oatmeal:

1. Classic Baked Oatmeal:

Ingredients:

2 cups rolled oats

1/2 cup brown sugar

1 teaspoon baking powder

1/2 teaspoon salt

1 teaspoon cinnamon

2 cups milk (or a dairy-free alternative)

1/2 cup applesauce (unsweetened)

2 eggs (or flaxseed eggs for a vegan option)

2 teaspoons vanilla extract

Instructions: Mix all the ingredients together and bake in a greased dish at 350°F (175°C) for 30-35 minutes until the top is golden brown.

2. Berry Bliss Baked Oatmeal:

Ingredients:

2 cups rolled oats

1/4 cup honey or maple syrup

1 teaspoon baking powder

1/2 teaspoon salt

1/2 teaspoon cinnamon

2 cups milk (or a dairy-free alternative)

1 cup mixed berries (blueberries, strawberries, raspberries)

1 teaspoon vanilla extract

Instructions:

Combine all the ingredients except the berries and pour the mixture into a greased dish. Sprinkle the mixed berries on top.

Bake at 350°F (175°C) for 30-35 minutes.

3. Apple Cinnamon Baked Oatmeal:

Ingredients:

2 cups rolled oats

1/4 cup brown sugar

1 teaspoon baking powder

1/2 teaspoon salt

1 teaspoon cinnamon

2 cups milk (or a dairy-free alternative)

1 cup diced apples (peeled and cored)

1/2 cup chopped nuts (such as walnuts or pecans, optional)

Instructions:

Combine all the ingredients and pour into a greased dish.

Bake at 350°F (175°C) for 30-35 minutes.

4. Banana Nut Baked Oatmeal:

Ingredients:

2 cups rolled oats

1/4 cup brown sugar

1 teaspoon baking powder

1/2 teaspoon salt

1/2 teaspoon cinnamon

2 cups milk (or a dairy-free alternative)

2 ripe bananas, mashed

1/2 cup chopped nuts (such as pecans or almonds)

Instructions:

Mix all the ingredients together and bake at 350°F (175°C) for 30-35 minutes.

5. pumpkin Baked Oatmeal:

Ingredients:

2 cups rolled oats

1/4 cup brown sugar

1 teaspoon baking powder

1/2 teaspoon salt

1 teaspoon pumpkin spice (or a mix of cinnamon, nutmeg, and cloves)

2 cups milk (or a dairy-free alternative)

1/2 cup canned pumpkin puree

1/2 cup chopped pecans or walnuts (optional)

Instructions:

Combine all the ingredients and bake at 350°F (175°C) for 30-35 minutes.

These baked oatmeal varieties can be adjusted to your preferences by adding or omitting ingredients. They are not only delicious but also a great way to incorporate fiber, whole grains, and various fruits and nuts into your breakfast routine during pregnancy. Enjoy experimenting with different flavors!

CHAPTER 5

Wholesome Lunchtime Favorites

5.1 Vibrant Salad Creations

Creating vibrant salads during pregnancy is an excellent way to nourish your body with essential nutrients while satisfying your taste buds. Here are five vibrant salad creations that are both nutritious and delicious:

1. Summer Berry Spinach Salad:

Ingredients:

Baby spinach leaves

Mixed berries (strawberries, blueberries, raspberries)

Sliced almonds or candied pecans

Crumbled feta cheese (optional)

Balsamic vinaigrette dressing

Instructions:Toss the spinach with the mixed berries, almonds or pecans, and feta cheese.

Drizzle with balsamic vinaigrette dressing for a sweet and tangy flavor.

2. Mediterranean Quinoa Salad:

Ingredients:

Cooked quinoa

Cherry tomatoes, halved

Cucumber, diced

Red onion, thinly sliced

Kalamata olives, pitted

Feta cheese crumbles

Fresh basil leaves

Lemon vinaigrette dressing

Instructions:

Combine cooked quinoa with cherry tomatoes, cucumber, red onion, olives, and feta cheese.

Garnish with fresh basil leaves and drizzle with lemon vinaigrette for a Mediterranean-inspired salad.

3. Asian-Inspired Rainbow Salad:

Ingredients:

Shredded red cabbage

Sliced bell peppers (red, yellow, or orange)

Shredded carrots

Edamame beans

Sliced scallions

Chopped cilantro

Sesame ginger dressing

Instructions:

Mix the shredded red cabbage, bell peppers, carrots, edamame beans, scallions, and cilantro.

Toss with sesame ginger dressing for a refreshing and crunchy salad.

4. Roasted Beet and Goat Cheese Salad:

Ingredients:

Roasted beets, sliced

Mixed greens (arugula, baby spinach, or mesclun)

Crumbled goat cheese

Chopped walnuts or pecans

Balsamic glaze or vinaigrette dressing

Instructions:

Arrange the roasted beet slices on a bed of mixed greens.

Top with crumbled goat cheese and chopped nuts.

Drizzle with balsamic glaze or vinaigrette for a sweet and earthy salad.

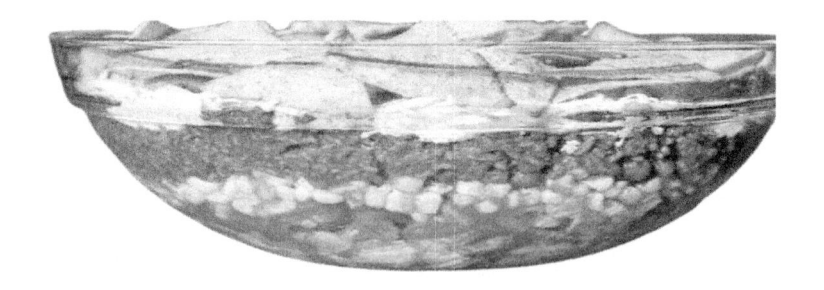

5. Tex-Mex Taco Salad:

Ingredients:

Romaine lettuce, chopped

Cooked black beans

Corn kernels (fresh or roasted)

Diced tomatoes

Sliced avocado

Shredded cheddar cheese

Crushed tortilla chips

Creamy avocado lime dressing

Instructions: Layer romaine lettuce with black beans, corn, tomatoes, avocado, and cheddar cheese.

Top with crushed tortilla chips and drizzle with creamy avocado lime dressing for a Tex-Mex twist.

These vibrant salad creations offer a variety of flavors, textures, and colors to keep your meals exciting and nutritious during pregnancy.

Feel free to adapt these salads to your dietary preferences and add protein sources like grilled chicken, tofu, or chickpeas for added sustenance.

5.2 Satisfying Sandwiches and Wraps

Satisfying sandwiches and wraps are a convenient and delicious way to enjoy a balanced meal during pregnancy. Here are some ideas for satisfying and nutritious sandwich and wrap creations:

1. Veggie Hummus Wrap:

Ingredients:

Whole-grain or spinach tortilla

Hummus

Sliced cucumber

Sliced bell peppers

Sliced tomatoes

Shredded carrots

Baby spinach or mixed greens

Instructions:

Spread a generous amount of hummus on the tortilla.

Layer the sliced veggies and greens.

Roll it up tightly and cut into halves for a satisfying wrap.

2. Turkey and Avocado Sandwich:

Ingredients:

Whole-grain bread or whole-grain wrap

Sliced turkey breast

Sliced avocado

Sliced tomatoes

Lettuce or spinach leaves

Dijon mustard or mayo (optional)

Instructions:

Layer the turkey, avocado, tomatoes, and greens on the bread or wrap.

Add a dollop of Dijon mustard or mayo for extra flavor if desired.

3. Caprese Panini:

Ingredients:

Ciabatta bread or whole-grain baguette

Fresh mozzarella cheese slices

Sliced tomatoes

Fresh basil leaves

Balsamic glaze

Instructions:

Assemble mozzarella, tomatoes, and basil leaves between slices of bread.

Press in a panini press or grill pan until the cheese is melted.

Drizzle with balsamic glaze before serving.

4. Chickpea Salad Wrap:

Ingredients:

Whole-grain or spinach tortilla

Chickpea salad (mashed chickpeas, diced celery, diced red onion, Greek yogurt or mayo, lemon juice, salt, and pepper)

Sliced cucumber

Baby spinach

Instructions:

Spoon chickpea salad onto the tortilla.

Add sliced cucumber and baby spinach.

Roll it up into a wrap.

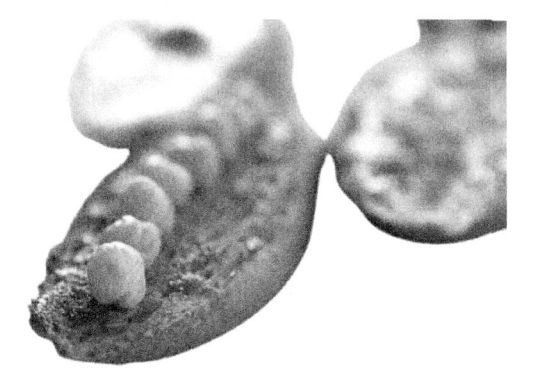

5. Grilled Veggie and Pesto Panini:

Ingredients:

Whole-grain bread or whole-grain wrap

Grilled or roasted vegetables (zucchini, eggplant, bell peppers)

Pesto sauce

Fresh mozzarella cheese slices (optional)

Instructions:

Layer the grilled veggies and cheese (if using) on the bread or wrap.

Spread pesto sauce on the other side.

Grill in a panini press until heated through and the bread is crispy.

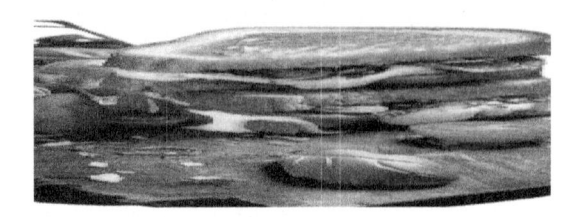

6. Tuna Salad Sandwich:

Ingredients:

Whole-grain bread or whole-grain wrap

Tuna salad (canned tuna, Greek yogurt or mayo, diced celery, diced pickles, lemon juice, salt, and pepper)

Sliced tomatoes

Lettuce leaves

Instructions:

Spread tuna salad on the bread or wrap.

Add sliced tomatoes and lettuce.

Enjoy a classic tuna sandwich.

These satisfying sandwich and wrap ideas are versatile and can be customized to suit your taste preferences and dietary needs during pregnancy.

Incorporate a variety of vegetables, lean proteins, and whole grains to ensure a balanced and nourishing meal.

5.3 Hearty Soups and Stews

Hearty soups and stews can provide comfort and essential nutrients during pregnancy. Here are some satisfying and nutritious soup and stew options for expecting mothers:

1. Lentil and Vegetable Soup:

Ingredients:

1 cup dried green or brown lentils, rinsed and drained

6 cups vegetable or chicken broth

Chopped carrots, celery, and onions

Chopped garlic

Diced tomatoes

Seasonings (such as thyme, bay leaves, and a bay leaf)

Salt and pepper to taste

Instructions:

Combine all ingredients in a large pot.

Bring to a boil, then reduce heat and simmer until lentils and vegetables are tender.

Remove bay leaves before serving.

2. Chicken and Rice Soup:

Ingredients:

Chicken breast or thigh, diced

Chicken broth

Chopped carrots, celery, and onions

Minced garlic

Cooked rice

Seasonings (such as parsley, dill, and black pepper)

Salt to taste

Instructions:

In a large pot, sauté chicken, garlic, and onions until chicken is no longer pink.

Add carrots, celery, and chicken broth.

Simmer until vegetables are tender, then stir in cooked rice and seasonings.

3. Minestrone Soup:

Ingredients:

Chopped onion, carrots, celery, and zucchini

Minced garlic

Diced tomatoes

Kidney beans or cannellini beans

Vegetable broth

Pasta (such as small shells or macaroni)

Fresh basil and parsley

Grated Parmesan cheese (optional)

Instructions: Sauté onions, carrots, celery, and garlic in olive oil until softened.

Add diced tomatoes, beans, and vegetable broth.

Bring to a boil, then add pasta and simmer until pasta is cooked.

Stir in fresh basil and parsley.

Serve with grated Parmesan cheese if desired.

4. Butternut Squash and Sweet Potato Stew:

Ingredients:

Cubed butternut squash and sweet potatoes

Chopped onions and garlic

Vegetable broth

Coconut milk

Curry powder, cumin, and cinnamon

Salt and pepper to taste

Instructions:

Sauté onions and garlic until fragrant.

Add butternut squash, sweet potatoes, vegetable broth, and spices.

Simmer until vegetables are tender, then stir in coconut milk.

Season with salt and pepper.

5. Tomato Basil Soup:

Ingredients:

Canned or fresh tomatoes

Chopped onions and garlic

Vegetable or chicken broth

Fresh basil leaves

Heavy cream or coconut milk (optional)

Salt and pepper to taste

Instructions: Sauté onions and garlic until translucent.

Add tomatoes, broth, and basil.

Simmer until tomatoes are soft, then blend until smooth.

Stir in cream or coconut milk if desired.

Season with salt and pepper.

These hearty soups and stews are not only comforting but also rich in nutrients, making them a great choice for pregnant women. Adjust the seasonings and ingredients to your taste and dietary preferences, and enjoy these nourishing meals during pregnancy.

CHAPTER 6

Nutrient-Rich Dinners for Two

6.1 Flavorful Pasta Dishes

Flavorful pasta dishes can be a delicious and satisfying choice during pregnancy. Here are some mouthwatering pasta recipes that you can enjoy:

1. Lemon Garlic Shrimp Pasta:

Ingredients:

Linguine or spaghetti

Shrimp, peeled and deveined

Olive oil

Minced garlic

Fresh lemon juice and zest

Fresh parsley

Salt and pepper to taste

Instructions:

Cook pasta according to package instructions.

In a skillet, sauté shrimp and garlic in olive oil until shrimp turn pink.

Toss cooked pasta with shrimp, lemon juice, lemon zest, and chopped parsley.

Season with salt and pepper.

2. Creamy Tomato Basil Pasta:

Ingredients:

Penne or fettuccine pasta

Olive oil

Chopped onions and garlic

Canned crushed tomatoes

Heavy cream or coconut milk

Fresh basil leaves

Grated Parmesan cheese (optional)

Instructions:

Cook pasta according to package instructions.

In a separate pan, sauté onions and garlic until fragrant.

Add crushed tomatoes and simmer for a few minutes.

Stir in cream or coconut milk and fresh basil.

Toss the cooked pasta in the sauce and top with grated Parmesan if desired

3. Spinach and Mushroom Alfredo Pasta:

Ingredients:

Fettuccine or bowtie pasta

Olive oil

Sliced mushrooms

Minced garlic

Baby spinach leaves

Alfredo sauce (store-bought or homemade)

Grated Parmesan cheese

Instructions:

Cook pasta according to package instructions.

Sauté mushrooms and garlic in olive oil until mushrooms are tender.

Add baby spinach and sauté until wilted.

Stir in Alfredo sauce and heat through.

Toss pasta with the sauce and top with grated Parmesan.

4. Pesto Pasta with Roasted Cherry Tomatoes:

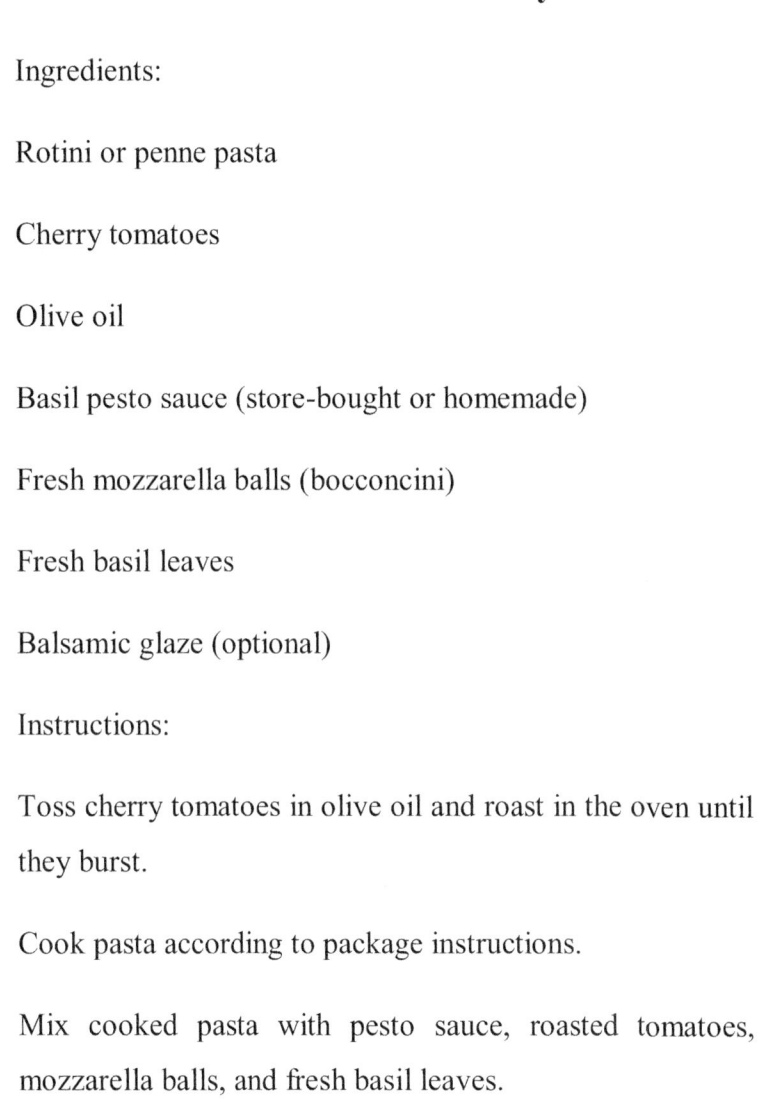

Ingredients:

Rotini or penne pasta

Cherry tomatoes

Olive oil

Basil pesto sauce (store-bought or homemade)

Fresh mozzarella balls (bocconcini)

Fresh basil leaves

Balsamic glaze (optional)

Instructions:

Toss cherry tomatoes in olive oil and roast in the oven until they burst.

Cook pasta according to package instructions.

Mix cooked pasta with pesto sauce, roasted tomatoes, mozzarella balls, and fresh basil leaves.

Drizzle with balsamic glaze if desired.

5. Vegetable Primavera with Garlic Butter Sauce:

Ingredients:

Spaghetti or linguine

Assorted vegetables (zucchini, bell peppers, cherry tomatoes, asparagus, etc.)

Butter

Minced garlic

Fresh lemon juice

Fresh parsley

Grated Parmesan cheese

Instructions: Cook pasta according to package instructions.

Sauté chopped vegetables in butter and garlic until tender-crisp.

Toss cooked pasta with the garlic butter sauce, lemon juice, fresh parsley, and grated Parmesan.

These flavorful pasta dishes offer a variety of tastes and textures to suit your cravings during pregnancy.

You can customize the ingredients and adjust seasonings to your liking. Enjoy these hearty pasta meals as a satisfying and nourishing part of your pregnancy diet.

6.2 Protein-Packed Entrees

Flavorful pasta dishes can be a delicious and satisfying choice during pregnancy. Here are some mouth watering pasta recipes that you can enjoy:

1. Lemon Garlic Shrimp Pasta:

Ingredients:

Linguine or spaghetti

Shrimp, peeled and deveined

Olive oil

Minced garlic

Fresh lemon juice and zest

Fresh parsley

Salt and pepper to taste

Instructions: Cook pasta according to package instructions.

In a skillet, sauté shrimp and garlic in olive oil until shrimp turn pink.

Toss cooked pasta with shrimp, lemon juice, lemon zest, and chopped parsley. Season with salt and pepper.

2. Creamy Tomato Basil Pasta:

Ingredients:

Penne or fettuccine pasta

Olive oil

Chopped onions and garlic

Canned crushed tomatoes

Heavy cream or coconut milk

Fresh basil leaves

Grated Parmesan cheese (optional)

Instructions:

Cook pasta according to package instructions.

In a separate pan, sauté onions and garlic until fragrant.

Add crushed tomatoes and simmer for a few minutes.

Stir in cream or coconut milk and fresh basil.

Toss the cooked pasta in the sauce and top with grated Parmesan if desired.

3. Spinach and Mushroom Alfredo Pasta:

Ingredients:

Fettuccine or bowtie pasta

Olive oil

Sliced mushrooms

Minced garlic

Baby spinach leaves

Alfredo sauce (store-bought or homemade)

Grated Parmesan cheese

Instructions:

Cook pasta according to package instructions.

Sauté mushrooms and garlic in olive oil until mushrooms are tender.

Add baby spinach and sauté until wilted.

Stir in Alfredo sauce and heat through.

Toss pasta with the sauce and top with grated Parmesan.

4. Pesto Pasta with Roasted Cherry Tomatoes:

Ingredients:

Rotini or penne pasta

Cherry tomatoes

Olive oil

Basil pesto sauce (store-bought or homemade)

Fresh mozzarella balls (bocconcini)

Fresh basil leaves

Balsamic glaze (optional)

Instructions:

Toss cherry tomatoes in olive oil and roast in the oven until they burst.

Cook pasta according to package instructions.

Mix cooked pasta with pesto sauce, roasted tomatoes, mozzarella balls, and fresh basil leaves.

Drizzle with balsamic glaze if desired.

5. Vegetable Primavera with Garlic Butter Sauce:

Ingredients:

Spaghetti or linguine

Assorted vegetables (zucchini, bell peppers, cherry tomatoes, asparagus, etc.)

Butter

Minced garlic

Fresh lemon juice

Fresh parsley

Grated Parmesan cheese

Instructions: Cook pasta according to package instructions.

Sauté chopped vegetables in butter and garlic until tender-crisp.

Toss cooked pasta with the garlic butter sauce, lemon juice, fresh parsley, and grated Parmesan.

These flavorful pasta dishes offer a variety of tastes and textures to suit your cravings during pregnancy. You can customize the ingredients and adjust seasonings to your liking. Enjoy these hearty pasta meals as a satisfying and nourishing part of your pregnancy diet.

6.2 Protein-Packed Entrees

Protein-packed entrees are essential during pregnancy to support your growing baby's development and your own health. Here are some protein-rich meal ideas:

1. Grilled Salmon with Lemon-Dill Sauce:

Ingredients:

Salmon fillets

Olive oil

Lemon juice and zest

Chopped fresh dill

Salt and pepper to taste

Instructions:

Brush salmon with olive oil and season with lemon zest, lemon juice, chopped dill, salt, and pepper.

Grill or bake until the salmon is cooked through.

Serve with additional lemon-dill sauce.

2. Tofu Stir-Fry:

Ingredients:

Extra-firm tofu, cubed

Mixed stir-fry vegetables (bell peppers, broccoli, carrots, snap peas, etc.)

Garlic and ginger, minced

Stir-fry sauce (soy sauce, sesame oil, and a touch of honey)

Cooked brown rice or quinoa

Instructions:

Sauté tofu in a hot wok or skillet until golden.

Add minced garlic and ginger, then toss in the mixed vegetables.

Stir in the stir-fry sauce.

Serve over cooked brown rice or quinoa.

3. Grilled Chicken Breast with Mango Salsa:

Ingredients:

Chicken breast

Olive oil

Paprika, cumin, and chili powder (for seasoning)

Ripe mango, diced

Diced red onion

Chopped fresh cilantro

Lime juice

Instructions:

Season chicken with olive oil, paprika, cumin, and chili powder.

Grill or bake until fully cooked.

Combine diced mango, red onion, cilantro, and lime juice for salsa.

Serve chicken topped with mango salsa.

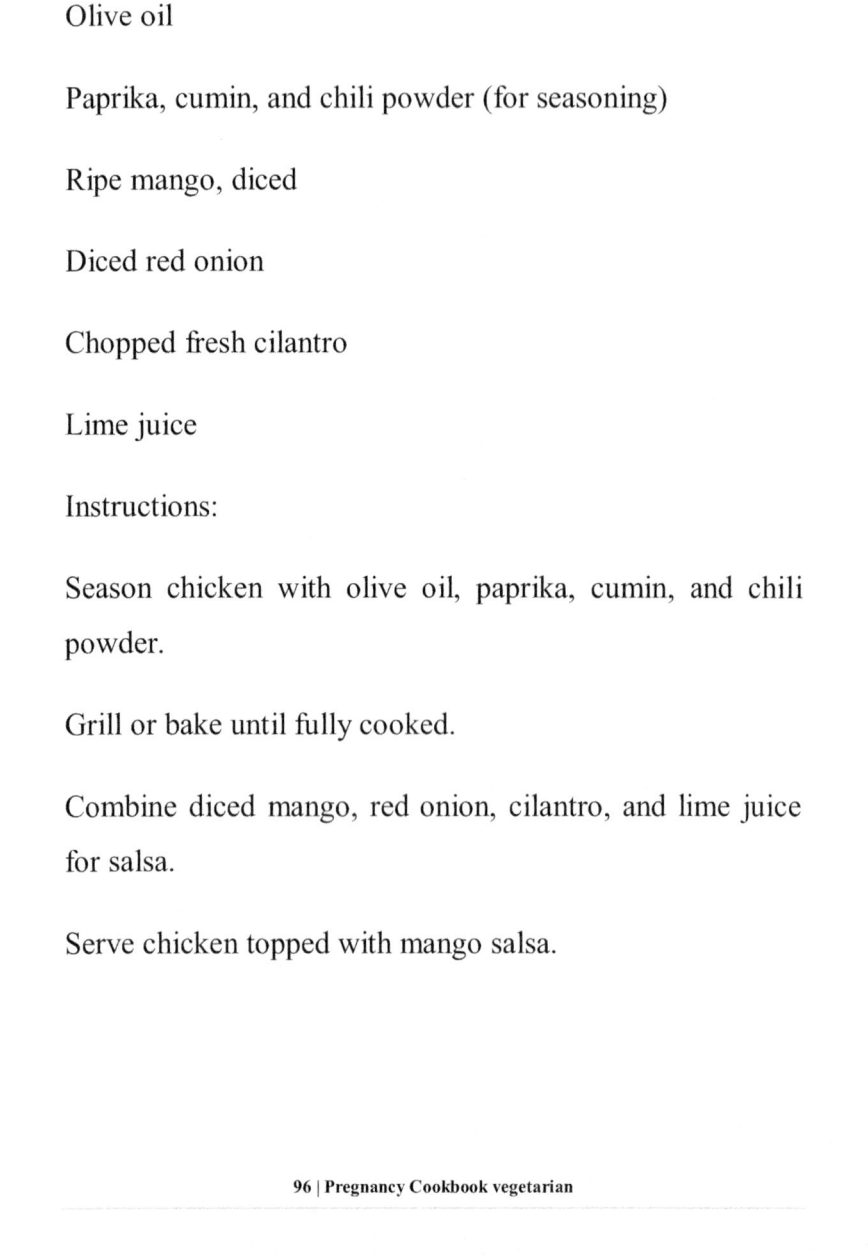

4. Lentil and Vegetable Curry:

Ingredients:

Green or brown lentils

Mixed vegetables (bell peppers, cauliflower, peas, etc.)

Curry paste or powder

Coconut milk

Chopped fresh cilantro

Instructions:

Cook lentils according to package instructions.

Sauté mixed vegetables in curry paste or powder.

Stir in cooked lentils and coconut milk.

Simmer until vegetables are tender.

Garnish with fresh cilantro and serve with rice.

5. Beef and Vegetable Stir-Fry:

Ingredients:

Thinly sliced beef strips

Soy sauce

Sesame oil

Minced garlic and ginger

Mixed stir-fry vegetables

Cooked rice or noodles

Instructions:

Marinate beef in soy sauce and sesame oil.

Sauté beef with garlic and ginger until cooked.

Add mixed vegetables and stir-fry until tender.

Serve over cooked rice or noodles.

These protein-packed entrees are not only delicious but also provide essential nutrients for a healthy pregnancy. Be sure to include a variety of protein sources in your diet, whether from animal or plant-based options, to meet your nutritional needs during this important time.

6.3 Veggie-Loaded Stir-Fries

Veggie-loaded stir-fries are a fantastic way to incorporate a variety of vegetables into your diet during pregnancy. They provide essential nutrients and are both delicious and satisfying. Here are some veggie-loaded stir-fry ideas:

1. Classic Vegetable Stir-Fry:

Ingredients:

Assorted vegetables (bell peppers, broccoli, snap peas, carrots, mushrooms, baby corn, etc.)

Tofu, tempeh, or edamame for added protein (optional)

Garlic and ginger, minced

Stir-fry sauce (soy sauce, sesame oil, and a touch of honey)

Cooked brown rice or quinoa

Instructions: Heat a wok or large skillet with oil.

Add minced garlic and ginger, followed by vegetables and protein (if using).

Stir-fry until vegetables are tender-crisp.

Toss with stir-fry sauce and serve over cooked brown rice or quinoa.

2. Spicy Thai Basil Stir-Fry:

Ingredients:

Assorted vegetables (bell peppers, green beans, Thai eggplant, etc.)

Thinly sliced chicken or tofu

Thai basil leaves

Red chili peppers, thinly sliced (adjust to taste)

Fish sauce (or soy sauce for a vegetarian option)

Palm sugar (or brown sugar)

Cooked jasmine rice

Instructions:

Sauté chicken or tofu until cooked through.

Add vegetables and red chili peppers, and stir-fry.

Stir in fish sauce and palm sugar, then toss in Thai basil leaves.

Serve with jasmine rice.

3. Garlic Sesame Bok Choy Stir-Fry:

Ingredients:

Baby bok choy, leaves separated

Sliced shiitake mushrooms

Minced garlic and ginger

Sesame oil

Soy sauce

Toasted sesame seeds

Instructions:

Sauté sliced mushrooms, garlic, and ginger in sesame oil.

Add baby bok choy leaves and stir-fry until wilted.

Season with soy sauce and top with toasted sesame seeds.

4. Mediterranean Chickpea Stir-Fry:

Ingredients:

Chickpeas, drained and rinsed

Chopped bell peppers, cherry tomatoes, and cucumbers

Chopped fresh parsley and mint

Lemon juice and olive oil dressing

Feta cheese (optional)

Instructions:

Mix chickpeas, bell peppers, cherry tomatoes, cucumbers, parsley, and mint.

Drizzle with lemon juice and olive oil dressing.

Add crumbled feta cheese if desired.

5. Sweet and Sour Vegetable Stir-Fry:

Ingredients:

Assorted vegetables (bell peppers, pineapple chunks, red onion, etc.)

Pineapple juice, vinegar, and brown sugar for the sauce

Tofu or tempeh (optional)

Cooked white or brown rice

Instructions:

Sauté tofu or tempeh (if using) until golden brown.

Add vegetables and stir-fry until tender.

Mix pineapple juice, vinegar, and brown sugar for the sauce and pour it over the stir-fry.

Serve over cooked rice.

These veggie-loaded stir-fry recipes offer a range of flavors and can be customized with your favorite vegetables and protein sources. They are a great way to get the nutrients you and your baby need during pregnancy while enjoying delicious and satisfying meals.

CHAPTER 7

Snacks and Small Bites

7.1 Quick and Healthy Snack Ideas

Quick and healthy snacks are essential during pregnancy to keep your energy levels stable and satisfy those cravings. Here are some nutritious snack ideas:

1. Greek Yogurt with Berries:

Top a bowl of Greek yogurt with fresh berries (blueberries, strawberries, or raspberries) for a protein-packed and antioxidant-rich snack.

2. Hummus and Veggies:

Pair hummus with sliced cucumbers, bell peppers, cherry tomatoes, or baby carrots for a crunchy and satisfying snack.

3. Apple Slices with Peanut Butter:

Spread natural peanut or almond butter on apple slices for a combination of fiber, healthy fats, and protein.

4. Trail Mix:

Create your own trail mix with a mix of nuts (almonds, walnuts, cashews), dried fruits (apricots, raisins, cranberries), and a touch of dark chocolate chips for a sweet and salty treat.

5. Cottage Cheese with Pineapple:

Enjoy a serving of cottage cheese with chunks of fresh pineapple for a snack rich in protein and vitamin C.

6. Hard-Boiled Eggs:

Prepare a batch of hard-boiled eggs and keep them in the fridge for a quick source of protein.

7. Avocado Toast:

Spread ripe avocado on whole-grain toast and sprinkle with a dash of salt and pepper for a creamy and satisfying snack.

8. Sliced Banana with Almond Butter:

Top banana slices with almond butter and a sprinkle of cinnamon for a sweet and nutty snack.

9. Veggie Sticks with Guacamole:

Dip sliced bell peppers, celery, or cucumber in homemade guacamole for a satisfying and veggie-rich snack.

10. Popcorn:

- Air-popped popcorn is a whole-grain snack that can be lightly seasoned with herbs, spices, or nutritional yeast for extra flavor.

11. Mini Caprese Skewers:

- Thread cherry tomatoes, fresh mozzarella balls, and basil leaves onto skewers, and drizzle with balsamic glaze for a delicious and refreshing snack.

12. Edamame:

- Steam edamame (young soybeans) and lightly sprinkle with sea salt for a protein-rich and savory snack.

13. Oatmeal with Nut Butter:

- Make a quick bowl of oatmeal and swirl in a spoonful of your favorite nut butter for a warm and satisfying snack.

14. Cucumber and Cream Cheese Sandwiches:

- Create mini cucumber sandwiches by spreading cream cheese between cucumber slices for a refreshing and creamy snack.

15. Rice Cakes with Cottage Cheese and Berries:

- Top rice cakes with cottage cheese and fresh berries for a light and filling snack.

Remember to stay hydrated and choose nutrient-dense snacks that provide a balance of protein, healthy fats, and fiber to keep you and your baby nourished during pregnancy.

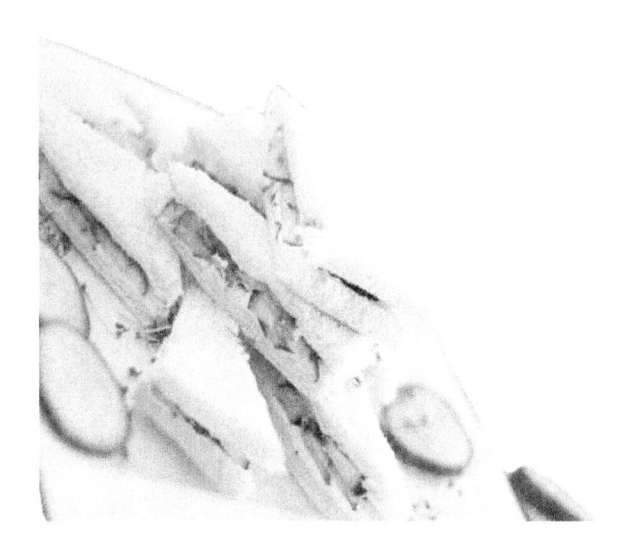

7.2 Homemade Energy Bars and Bites

Homemade energy bars and bites are a nutritious and convenient snack option for pregnant women. They can provide you with sustained energy and essential nutrients. Here are some delicious recipes to try:

1. No-Bake Nut and Date Energy Bars:

Ingredients:

1 cup pitted dates

1/2 cup almonds

1/2 cup walnuts

1/4 cup rolled oats

2 tablespoons chia seeds

2 tablespoons honey or maple syrup

1/2 teaspoon vanilla extract

Instructions:

In a food processor, blend dates, almonds, walnuts, oats, and chia seeds until finely chopped.

Add honey or maple syrup and vanilla extract, and blend until the mixture starts to come together.

Press the mixture into a lined baking dish and refrigerate for a few hours before cutting into bars.

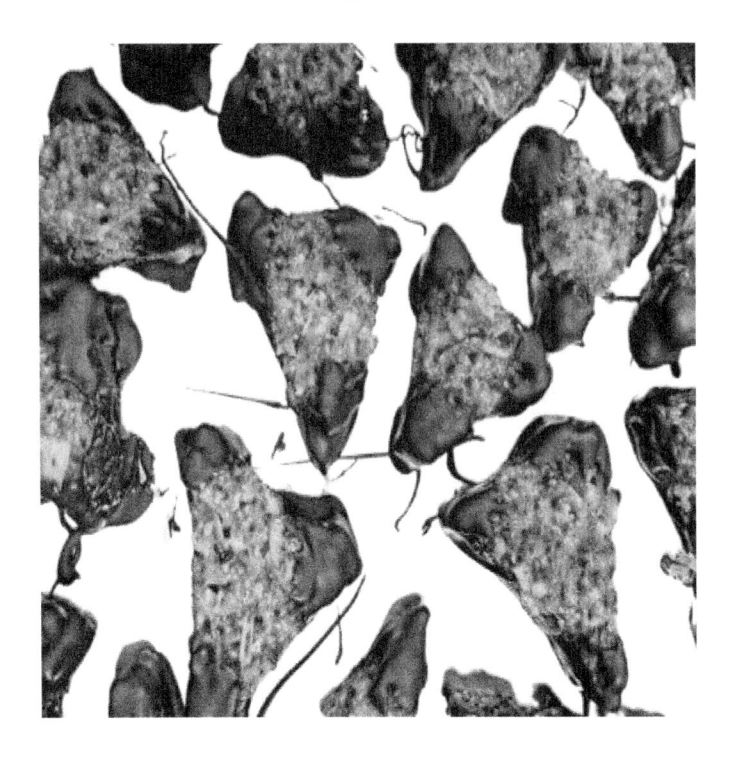

2. Peanut Butter and Chocolate Energy Bites:

Ingredients:

1 cup rolled oats

1/2 cup creamy peanut butter

1/3 cup honey

1/4 cup ground flaxseed

1/4 cup unsweetened cocoa powder

1/2 cup mini chocolate chips

1 teaspoon vanilla extract

Instructions:

In a large bowl, mix oats, peanut butter, honey, ground flaxseed, cocoa powder, chocolate chips, and vanilla extract until well combined.

Refrigerate the mixture for about 30 minutes to make it easier to handle.

Roll the mixture into bite-sized balls and place them on a parchment-lined tray.

Chill in the refrigerator until they firm up.

3. Cranberry Almond Energy Bars:

Ingredients:

1 1/2 cups dried cranberries

1 cup almonds

1/4 cup pumpkin seeds

1/4 cup rolled oats

1/4 cup almond butter

2 tablespoons honey

1/2 teaspoon cinnamon

Instructions:

In a food processor, combine dried cranberries, almonds, pumpkin seeds, oats, almond butter, honey, and cinnamon.

Pulse until the mixture forms a sticky dough.

Press the mixture into a lined baking dish and refrigerate until set. Cut into bars.

4. Apricot and Cashew Energy Bites:

Ingredients:

1 cup dried apricots

1/2 cup cashews

1/4 cup shredded coconut

1/4 cup rolled oats

1 tablespoon honey

1/2 teaspoon vanilla extract

Instructions: Blend dried apricots, cashews, shredded coconut, oats, honey, and vanilla extract in a food processor until a sticky mixture forms.

Roll the mixture into small balls and place them on a baking sheet.

Chill in the refrigerator until firm.

These homemade energy bars and bites are not only delicious but also packed with essential nutrients and natural sweetness. They make for a great snack to satisfy your cravings and provide you with the energy you need during pregnancy.

CHAPTER 8

Sweet Treats for Expecting Moms

8.1 Dessert Options without Guilt

Enjoying guilt-free desserts during pregnancy can be a delightful way to satisfy your sweet tooth while maintaining a balanced diet. Here are some dessert options that are both delicious and nutritious:

1. Fruit Salad with Honey-Lime Drizzle:

Combine a variety of fresh fruits like berries, melon, pineapple, and citrus.

Drizzle with a mixture of honey and freshly squeezed lime juice for a naturally sweet and tangy dessert.

2. Greek Yogurt Parfait:

Layer Greek yogurt with fresh berries, a drizzle of honey, and a sprinkle of granola for a creamy and satisfying dessert.

3. Baked Apples with Cinnamon and Walnuts:

Core apples and fill with a mixture of chopped walnuts, cinnamon, and a touch of honey.

Bake until tender for a warm and comforting treat.

4. Chocolate-Dipped Strawberries:

Dip fresh strawberries in dark chocolate for a decadent yet relatively healthy dessert.

Dark chocolate contains antioxidants and can satisfy your chocolate cravings.

5. Frozen Banana Bites:

Slice bananas into bite-sized pieces and dip them in melted dark chocolate.

Freeze until the chocolate hardens, creating a sweet and satisfying frozen treat.

6. Chia Seed Pudding:

Mix chia seeds with almond milk or coconut milk and a touch of honey or maple syrup.

Let it sit in the fridge until it thickens, then top with fresh fruit or nuts.

7. Oatmeal Raisin Cookies:

Make oatmeal raisin cookies using whole-grain oats, raisins, and a reduced amount of sugar.

You can even substitute some of the sugar with unsweetened applesauce for natural sweetness.

8. Frozen Yogurt Bark:

Spread Greek yogurt on a baking sheet, and sprinkle it with fresh fruit, nuts, and a drizzle of honey.

Freeze until firm, then break it into pieces for a refreshing dessert.

9. Mini Fruit Tarts:

Create mini fruit tarts using whole-grain tart shells, a layer of Greek yogurt, and a variety of fresh fruit on top.

Drizzle with a touch of honey for added sweetness.

10. Dark Chocolate Covered Almonds:

- Dip almonds in melted dark chocolate and let them cool until the chocolate hardens.

- These provide a satisfying crunch and a hint of sweetness.

11. Coconut Bliss Balls:

- Mix shredded coconut, almond butter, a touch of honey, and a pinch of sea salt.

Roll the mixture into bite-sized balls and refrigerate until firm.

These guilt-free dessert options are designed to satisfy your sweet cravings while providing essential nutrients and maintaining a balanced diet during pregnancy. Remember to enjoy them in moderation as part of your overall meal plan.

8.2 Decadent Fruit-Based Sweets

Indulging in decadent fruit-based sweets during pregnancy can satisfy your cravings for something sweet while still providing essential nutrients. Here are some delicious fruit-based dessert options:

1. Grilled Pineapple with Cinnamon and Honey:

Slice fresh pineapple and grill until it caramelizes slightly.

Sprinkle with cinnamon and drizzle with honey for a warm and naturally sweet treat.

2. Mango Sorbet:

Puree ripe mangoes and freeze the mixture to make homemade mango sorbet.

It's a refreshing and guilt-free way to enjoy the natural sweetness of mango.

3. Berry Parfait with Whipped Coconut Cream:

Layer mixed berries (strawberries, blueberries, raspberries) with whipped coconut cream for a luscious and dairy-free dessert.

4. Chocolate-Covered Frozen Bananas:

Slice bananas into bite-sized pieces, dip them in melted dark chocolate, and freeze until the chocolate hardens for a satisfying frozen treat.

5. Watermelon Pizza:

Cut a thick slice of watermelon and top it with Greek yogurt, fresh berries, and a drizzle of honey for a fruity "pizza."

6. Stuffed Baked Apples:

Core apples and stuff them with a mixture of chopped nuts, dried fruits, cinnamon, and a touch of honey or maple syrup.

Bake until the apples are tender and the filling is caramelized.

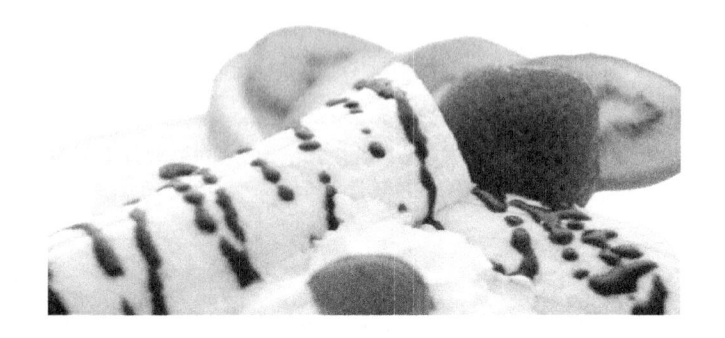

7. Strawberry Cheesecake Bites:

Blend fresh strawberries with cream cheese and a touch of honey.

Pipe or spoon the mixture onto graham cracker squares for mini cheesecake bites.

8. Frozen Grapes Dipped in Dark Chocolate:

Freeze grapes and then dip them in melted dark chocolate.

The contrast between the frozen grape and the rich chocolate is delightful.

9. Banana Ice Cream:

Freeze ripe bananas and blend them until creamy for a banana "ice cream."

Add cocoa powder, peanut butter, or honey for extra flavor.

10. Baked Peaches with Almonds:

- Halve peaches and remove the pits.

- Fill the hollow with almond butter and sprinkle with chopped almonds.

- Bake until the peaches are tender and the almond butter is slightly caramelized.

11. Fruit Kabobs with Yogurt Dip:

- Skewer fresh fruit chunks (melon, kiwi, berries, pineapple) and serve with a side of vanilla yogurt for dipping.

12. Raspberry Chia Seed Pudding:

- Mix fresh or frozen raspberries with chia seeds and almond milk.

- Let it sit in the fridge until it thickens for a fruity chia seed pudding.

These decadent fruit-based sweets are both satisfying and nutritious, making them a great choice for pregnancy. They allow you to enjoy the natural sweetness of fruits while indulging in a delightful dessert.

CHAPTER 9

Staying Hydrated with Pregnancy-Friendly Drinks

9.1 Infused Water and Herbal Teas

Staying hydrated is crucial during pregnancy, and infused water and herbal teas are excellent options for adding flavor and variety to your hydration routine. Here are some refreshing infused water ideas and safe herbal teas to enjoy during pregnancy:

Infused Water:

Citrus Bliss: Squeeze lemon, lime, and orange slices into a pitcher of cold water. Add a few sprigs of fresh mint for a burst of flavor.

Cucumber and Mint: Slice cucumber and add it to a pitcher of water along with fresh mint leaves. Let it infuse for a refreshing and hydrating drink.

Berry Medley: Combine a mix of fresh or frozen berries (strawberries, blueberries, raspberries) with water. You can also add a twist of lime or lemon for extra zing.

Pineapple and Ginger: Add pineapple chunks and a few slices of fresh ginger to water for a tropical and soothing infused drink.

Watermelon and Basil: Blend watermelon and a handful of basil leaves, then mix it with water for a light and hydrating infusion.

Lemon and Cucumber: Slice lemons and cucumbers and combine them in water with a pinch of salt for a refreshing drink.

Herbal Teas:

It's essential to choose herbal teas that are safe during pregnancy. Always consult with your healthcare provider before introducing new teas into your diet. Here are some generally considered safe options:

Peppermint Tea: Peppermint tea can help relieve indigestion and nausea, common symptoms during pregnancy. It's best enjoyed in moderation.

Ginger Tea: Ginger tea is known for its soothing effects on nausea and digestive discomfort. It's a popular choice among pregnant women.

Chamomile Tea: Chamomile tea may help with relaxation and sleep, but it should be consumed in moderation due to its potential to cause uterine contractions.

Raspberry Leaf Tea: Raspberry leaf tea is often recommended during the third trimester as it may help prepare the uterus for labor. Consult your healthcare provider before using it.

Lemon Balm Tea: Lemon balm tea is a mild and pleasant option known for its calming effects, which can be beneficial during pregnancy.

Nettle Tea: Nettle tea is a source of essential nutrients like iron and calcium. It's generally considered safe and nutritious during pregnancy.

Rooibos Tea: Rooibos tea is caffeine-free and rich in antioxidants. It's a popular choice for expectant mothers looking for a caffeine-free alternative.

Dandelion Tea: Dandelion tea may have diuretic properties and can be consumed in moderation for its potential benefits.

Remember that moderation is key when it comes to herbal teas during pregnancy, and it's essential to consult with your healthcare provider to ensure that the teas you choose are safe for your specific situation. Staying well-hydrated and enjoying these flavorful infused waters and herbal teas can enhance your overall pregnancy experience.

9.2 Pregnancy Smoothies

Pregnancy smoothies are a tasty and convenient way to pack essential nutrients into your diet while expecting. These smoothie recipes can provide vitamins, minerals, and energy to support both you and your growing baby. Here are some pregnancy-friendly smoothie ideas:

1. Berry Blast Smoothie:

Ingredients:

1 cup mixed berries (strawberries, blueberries, raspberries)

1 ripe banana

1/2 cup Greek yogurt

1/2 cup spinach (for added folate)

1 tablespoon honey or maple syrup

1/2 cup almond milk

Ice cubes (optional)

Instructions:

Blend all the ingredients until smooth and creamy.

Adjust the sweetness with honey or maple syrup as needed.

2. Tropical Delight Smoothie:

Ingredients:

1 cup fresh or frozen mango chunks

1/2 cup fresh or frozen pineapple chunks

1/2 ripe banana

1/2 cup Greek yogurt

1/2 cup coconut milk

1 tablespoon chia seeds (for added omega-3 fatty acids)

Instructions:

Blend all the ingredients until well combined.

Add more coconut milk if you prefer a thinner consistency.

3. Green Power Smoothie:

Ingredients:

1 cup spinach

1/2 ripe avocado

1/2 banana

1/2 cup Greek yogurt

1 tablespoon honey or maple syrup

1/2 cup water or coconut water

Ice cubes (optional)

Instructions:

Blend spinach, avocado, banana, and Greek yogurt until smooth.

Add honey or maple syrup for sweetness and water or coconut water for desired thickness.

4. Peanut Butter and Banana Smoothie:

Ingredients:

1 ripe banana

2 tablespoons natural peanut butter (unsweetened)

1/2 cup Greek yogurt

1/2 cup milk (dairy or plant-based)

1 tablespoon flaxseed meal (for added fiber)

Instructions:

Blend banana, peanut butter, Greek yogurt, and milk until creamy.

Stir in flaxseed meal for added nutrition.

5. Orange Creamsicle Smoothie:

Ingredients:

1 ripe orange, peeled and segmented

1/2 cup Greek yogurt

1/2 cup coconut milk or almond milk

1 tablespoon honey or maple syrup

Ice cubes (optional)

Instructions:

Blend orange segments, Greek yogurt, and coconut or almond milk until smooth.

Add honey or maple syrup for sweetness and ice cubes for a colder drink.

These pregnancy smoothie recipes offer a balance of essential nutrients and flavors to keep you energized and satisfied during this special time. Feel free to customize them to your taste and dietary preferences while ensuring you're meeting your nutritional needs.

CHAPTER 11

Resources and Further Reading

11.1 Recommended Cookbooks

There are several highly regarded cookbooks that cater to the needs of expectant mothers, providing nutritious and delicious recipes suitable for pregnancy. Here are some recommended cookbooks for pregnant women:

1. "Eating Well When You're Expecting" by Heidi Murkoff:

Author Heidi Murkoff, known for the "What to Expect When You're Expecting" series, offers a cookbook filled with recipes designed to meet the nutritional needs of expectant mothers. It includes meal plans, shopping lists, and dietary guidance.

2. "The Whole 9 Months: A Week-By-Week Pregnancy Nutrition Guide with Recipes for a Healthy Start" by Jennifer Lang, MD, and Dana Angelo White, MS, RD:

This cookbook provides week-by-week guidance for a healthy pregnancy diet, accompanied by nutritious recipes that correspond to each stage of pregnancy.

3. "The Pregnancy Cookbook: 25 Quick & Easy Recipes to Feed Your Baby Bump" by Annie Marshall:

Annie Marshall's cookbook focuses on easy and quick recipes tailored for pregnant women. It includes dishes that are flavorful and convenient for busy expectant mothers.

4. "The Well-Rounded Pregnancy Cookbook: Give Your Baby a Healthy Start with 100 Recipes That Adapt to Fit How You Feel" by Karen Gurwitz, RDN, and Jen Hoy:

This cookbook offers adaptable recipes that cater to various pregnancy symptoms and cravings. It emphasizes the importance of flexibility in meal planning.

5. "Real Baby Food: Easy, All-Natural Recipes for Your Baby and Toddler" by Jenna Helwig:

Although this book primarily focuses on baby food, it includes a section on pregnancy nutrition and provides insights into transitioning from pregnancy to introducing solid foods to your baby.

6. "Nourishing Meals: Healthy Gluten-Free Recipes for the Whole Family" by Alissa Segersten and Tom Malterre MS CN:

While not exclusively a pregnancy cookbook, this resource offers a wealth of gluten-free recipes that can be adapted for expectant mothers with dietary restrictions.

7. "The Healthy Pregnancy Cookbook: Eating Twice as Well for a Healthy Baby" by Jane Middleton:

Jane Middleton's cookbook emphasizes eating nutritious and wholesome foods during pregnancy, offering recipes that are both health-conscious and delicious.

These cookbooks can be valuable resources for pregnant women looking to maintain a balanced and nutritious diet throughout their pregnancy journey. Always consult with your healthcare provider or a registered dietitian to ensure that your dietary choices align with your specific nutritional needs during pregnancy.

11.2 Online Resources for Vegetarian Moms

Online resources can be incredibly helpful for vegetarian moms during pregnancy. They provide information, recipes, and support for maintaining a healthy and balanced vegetarian diet. Here are some recommended online resources for vegetarian moms:

1. Vegetarian Nutrition:

This website, run by the Academy of Nutrition and Dietetics, offers evidence-based information and resources on vegetarian and vegan nutrition. It's an excellent source for understanding the dietary needs of vegetarian moms.

2. The Vegetarian Resource Group:

The Vegetarian Resource Group provides a wealth of information on vegetarian and vegan diets. They offer articles, recipes, nutrition facts, and guidance for pregnant vegetarians.

3. American Pregnancy Association:

The American Pregnancy Association has a section on their website that provides guidance on nutrition during pregnancy, including tips for vegetarian and vegan mothers.

4. Vegetarian Times:

Vegetarian Times offers a variety of vegetarian and vegan recipes, including those suitable for pregnant women. They also have articles on pregnancy nutrition and wellness.

5. The Vegan Society:

The Vegan Society's website includes a section on vegan nutrition during pregnancy. It provides guidance and resources for maintaining a healthy vegan diet while expecting.

6. Oh She Glows:

Oh She Glows is a popular vegan food blog with a pregnancy and postpartum section that includes vegan pregnancy tips, recipes, and personal stories.

7. NutritionFacts.org:

Run by Dr. Michael Greger, NutritionFacts.org provides evidence-based nutrition information, including videos and articles on pregnancy nutrition for vegetarians and vegans.

8. Plant-Based Juniors:

Plant-Based Juniors focuses on plant-based nutrition for families, including pregnancy and children. They offer resources, recipes, and expert advice for vegetarian and vegan parents.

9. VegKitchen:

VegKitchen features a dedicated section on pregnancy and vegan diets. It provides articles, recipes, and tips for pregnant vegetarians and vegans.

10. The Balanced Vegetarian:

- This website offers a range of vegetarian and vegan recipes that are suitable for pregnant women. It also provides information on pregnancy nutrition.

Remember that it's essential to consult with a healthcare provider or registered dietitian when making significant dietary changes during pregnancy, especially if you're following a vegetarian or vegan diet. They can provide personalized guidance to ensure you meet your nutritional needs for a healthy pregnancy.

Printed in Great Britain
by Amazon